ICELAND

TIGER BOOKS INTERNATIONAL

Text
Fabio Bourbon

Layout
Anna Galliani

Map
Cristina Franco

Translation
Barbara Fisher

Contents

1 *A stern-looking statue of Leifur Eiríksson, the legendary Icelandic navigator who in the 10th century reached the coasts of North America, stands before the Hallgrímskirkja, the modern cathedral that dominates the Reykjavík skyline.*

2-3 *The immense terminal crevasse of Breidamerkujökull, a tongue of Vatnajökull, the largest glacier in Europe, breaks in the iceberg-filled waters of Jökulsárlón.*

4-5 *A moonscape dotted with steaming vents and boiling mudpots greets those who venture into Leirhnjúkur, inside the volcanic area of Krafla, a few miles from Lake Myvatn.*

6-7 *Although caught in the formidable grip of the freezing winter, the Dettifoss waterfall offers an impressive spectacle; not even the polar winter temperatures of the central northern highland can totally tame its fury.*

8 *In winter Reykjavík lies beneath a white mantle; although by no means temperate, the climate of the Icelandic capital is less rigid than would be expected. Thanks to the effects of the Gulf Stream, the city's mean temperature in January is 6.1 F, higher than that of many other European cities.*

9 *Iceland is a young nation and not only because it gained independence in the not so distant 1944; it has one of the highest birth rates in Europe.*

This edition published in 1998 by TIGER BOOKS INTERNATIONAL PLC , 26a York Street Twickenham TW1 3LJ, England.

First published by Edizioni White Star. Title of the original edition: Islanda, volto di ghiaccio, cuore di fuoco. © World copyright 1998 by Edizioni White Star, Via Candido Sassone 22/24, 13100 Vercelli, Italy.

ISBN 1-84056-023-1

Printed in Singapore by Tien Wah Press. Colour separations by Fotomec, Turin.

The Publisher would like to thank the Iceland Tourism Board for the kind cooperation during the realization of this book.

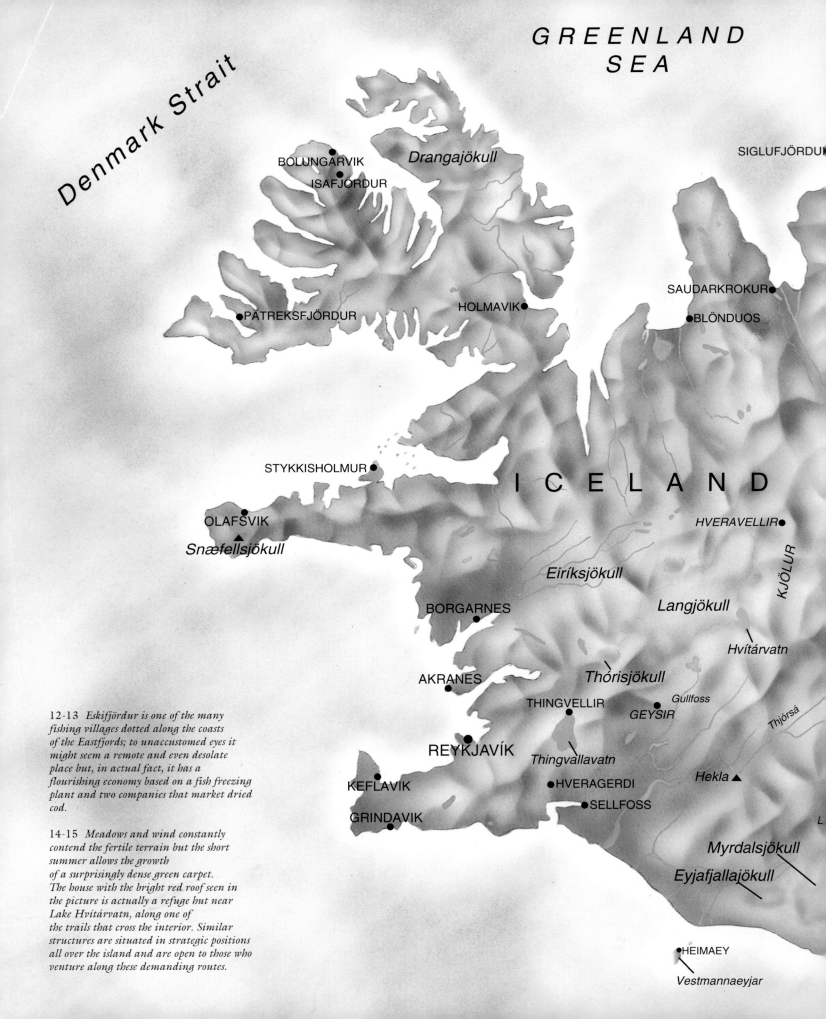

GREENLAND
SEA

Denmark Strait

SIGLUFJÖRDUR

BOLUNGARVIK
ISAFJÖRDUR

Drangajökull

SAUDARKROKUR
BLÖNDUOS

PATREKSFJÖRDUR

HOLMAVIK

I C E L A N D

STYKKISHOLMUR

HVERAVELLIR

OLAFSVIK
▲
Snæfellsjökull

Eiríksjökull

Langjökull

KJÖLUR

Hvítárvatn

BORGARNES

Thórisjökull

AKRANES

THINGVELLIR

Gullfoss

GEYSIR

Thjórsá

12-13 *Eskifjördur is one of the many
fishing villages dotted along the coasts
of the Eastfjords; to unaccustomed eyes it
might seem a remote and even desolate
place but, in actual fact, it has a
flourishing economy based on a fish freezing
plant and two companies that market dried
cod.*

REYKJAVÍK

Thingvallavatn

Hekla ▲

KEFLAVIK

HVERAGERDI

SELLFOSS

GRINDAVIK

14-15 *Meadows and wind constantly
contend the fertile terrain but the short
summer allows the growth
of a surprisingly dense green carpet.
The house with the bright red roof seen in
the picture is actually a refuge hut near
Lake Hvítárvatn, along one of
the trails that cross the interior. Similar
structures are situated in strategic positions
all over the island and are open to those who
venture along these demanding routes.*

Myrdalsjökull

Eyjafjallajökull

L

HEIMAEY

Vestmannaeyjar

KOPASKER

THORSHÖFN

SFJÖRDUR

HUSAVÍK

LVIK

Dettifoss

KRAFLA

VOPNAFJÖRDUR

Myvatn

AKUREYRI

Jökúlsá á Fjollum

Jökulsá á Dal

SEYDISFJÖRDUR

Herdubreid

EGILSSTADIR

NESKAUPSTADUR

ESKIFJÖRDUR

Jökulsá

Jökulsá

ODADAHRAUN

▲*Askja*

Hofsjökull

Tungnafellsjökull

DJUPIVOGUR

SPRENGISANDUR

Vatnajökull

HÖFN

hórisvatn

LAKAGIGAR

ALAUGAR

Jökulsárlón

RKJUBÆJARKLAUSTUR

ATLANTIC OCEAN

Introduction

Iceland is cold, bleak and a long way away.
A remote island out in the middle of the Atlantic, between Europe and America, where no trees grow and it rains all the time. A land of fire and ice, populated by people who speak an unintelligible language, as harsh and irksome as are the Icelanders themselves, descendants of the Vikings: tight-lipped, taciturn fishermen, fond of a drink like most Scandinavians. If anyone should ever describe Iceland to you like this, don't believe a single word.

They are probably speaking from hearsay and will delight in overdoing the "special effects". Perhaps they are repeating what they were told by an acquaintance who once visited the States - or Europe, depending on where you happen to be when you read this book - and the plane stopped to refuel at Keflavík airport on one of those days when the Icelandic sky looks as if it is made of slate and the clouds relentlessly discharge sleet without respite. I can imagine how people would feel. From the windows of the plane they can see a shiny, concrete runway creating a sharp, surrealistic contrast with the acid green grass that obstinately pushes up through the surrounding outcrops of lava; between one downpour and another they can only just, in the distance, make out the broken outline of a pitch-black mountain, oozing rivers of water. "Only madmen or bears could live in a hole like this" is the sole thought that comes to mind, then in a flash a ragged cloud swallows up the little landscape they had been allowed. After having refuelled, the jet takes off amidst a whirl of erratic drops and they are smugly satisfied to have chosen Miami or the Costa Smeralda for their holidays. What they will never know is that ten minutes later, like a sleepy giant, Iceland will shake off a good few of those clouds and produce splendid sunshine. In no time at all, the porous ground absorbs the rain, the tall grass is gently combed by the wind and the sky turns so blue that it will hurt your eyes, as it offers crazy contrasts with the saffron-yellow, ochre, plum, orange and red of the freshly-washed volcanic clay. The fortunate few that have remained at Keflavík - "the brave" equipped with backpack and sleeping bag as well as the more traditional tourists who have already reserved a comfortable hotel room in Reykjavík - will admire the spectacle and know they made the right decision: the coming days, be they many or few, will be unforgettable. Once back home, the sensation that they have had a special experience, seen an enchanted, wild and beautiful land will never leave them. Years later, images that remain breath-taking, stunning, exciting and, at the same time, slightly veiled by the sadness that often accompanies the memory of a loved one now far away, will appear suddenly and vividly before their eyes, as if time had stood still. It may be illogical to miss places and people - who know nothing about you - encountered only briefly, but the fact is that this land, with its icy face and fiery heart, possesses an air of magic no less real than the air you breathe, invisible yet there. It is easy, indeed inevitable, to fall immediately in love with Iceland: far more difficult is to turn your back and stay away for long. If you think this unlikely, bombastic or exaggerated, then leaf through these pages, observe the primeval landscapes, unleash your imagination and let the pictures speak. If you can listen to what they have to say, then you have been touched: the lava fields of Landmannalaugar glistening with a thousand streaks of obsidian and the solfataras of Hveravellir enveloped in the vapours of geothermal springs, multicoloured, impulsive and so out of place, there in the middle of the great central highland, between the Langjökull and Hofsjökull glaciers; then comes the immense moonscape of the coal-black desert that stretches out seventy or so miles from Egilstadir, the red Martian hills of Namaskardh and the impossibly blue icebergs that drift on the silent waters of the Jökulsárlón; the explosive spray of Strokkur, the most systematic geyser in Iceland and the rainbow on the Gullfoss falls, a celebration of

16 *The south-east part of this restless island continues to present an open wound through which, in 1783, the Laki fissure erupted thirty billion tons of lava over a period of 10 months.*

17 top *The famous Blue Lagoon, on the Reykjanes peninsula, is the result of the exploitation of the geothermal energy, that which also satisfies most of the country's requirements. This lovely little warm-water lake is formed by the used thermal water discharged by the Svartsengi power plant.*

17 bottom *On a clear sunny day, the Gullfoss falls show that they are one of Iceland's greatest natural wonders: here the turbulent waters of the Hvítá river hurtle 120 feet down from basaltic terraces, inside a deep canyon that lacerates the plateau.*

18-19 *Harsh and rugged in appearance, the coast near Höfn is a formidable sight. A similar view can only arouse wonder at the character of the first navigators to come within sight of this island, more than a thousand years ago. What incredible determination must have driven the Irish monks and shortly afterwards the Vikings from Norway. Iceland was then the edge of the world and an Ocean crossing meant defying freezing winds and treacherous currents on mere nutshells. It is only natural that today's islanders should betray a resolute nature.*

20-21 *Huge icebergs slowly plough the waters of Jökulsárlón, the lake that formed 50 or so years ago when telluric tremors closed the glacier's outlet to the sea. Iceland is an eternally young and totally unpredictable country and it is impossible to say whether or not in the next few years this stretch of water, 525 feet deep, will remain a fixed part of the scenery in the south of the island. In the meantime, this natural wonder is one of the greatest attractions in Iceland.*

iridescent vapours that still deserve their name, the Golden Falls. Observe all the colours of the sky and the green of the pastures; feel the warm sun on the black Vík cliffs and the biting wind that blows from the immense Vatnajökull ice-cap; breathe the intoxicating sense of total freedom given by the vast expanses of Skaftafell; see the tidy, clean, cheerful and happily informal atmosphere of Reykjavík or Akureyri; search the faces of the Icelanders, so reserved and yet so affable, helpful and sincere. This is no cold, inhospitable land. The impending field of low pressure mentioned in every weather forecast and the news of earthquakes and terrible volcanic eruptions - such as that of October 1996 which caused over three cubic kilometres of ice to melt with the subsequent overflowing of Lake Grímsvötn - give an alarming impression. Yet, however spellbinding and spectacular the occasional reports of news programmes in many parts of the world when similar cataclysms occur, they paint an abstract, unreal picture. Those wanting to at least scratch the surface of matters, to gain an initial understanding of the subtle alchemy that pervades this extraordinarily unusual corner of the world, really must sweep aside many clichés. Straddling the sixty-fifth parallel, on the edge of the Arctic Sea, Iceland has a far milder climate than its geographic position would suggest; thanks to the Gulf Stream which, after flowing along the coasts of America, heads north-east, mixing its waters with those of the north equatorial current, a branch of which even flows around the island, enclosing it in a tepid embrace. It is also true that even in summer, weather conditions are highly variable and totally unpredictable, especially in the south, but there is no need to exaggerate: seeing the disheartened expression on the face of a tourist caught in the umpteenth downpour, any Icelander will respond with some witticism. "If you don't like this weather, you need only wait two minutes" is predictably one of the most popular.

Freakish skies apart, the average temperature on summer afternoons is around 51 °F - although some days are decidedly warmer - and the winter averages are similar to those of New York or Vienna. Iceland has anything but an impossible climate, especially when you consider that the northernmost tip of the island almost touches the Arctic Circle and that, at the same latitude, Greenland is entirely covered with ice. Moreover,

fog is an almost unknown phenomenon in Iceland, the air is incredibly clear and smog simply does not exist, nor do the lethal acid rains now common to the entire industrialised world; to complete the picture it must be said that the sun never sets between the middle of May and the middle of August - and those who have witnessed the midnight sun just once know what a thrill it gives. In autumn and early winter the long arctic nights are not infrequently illuminated by the magic glimmer of the Aurora Borealis. Once established that no one freezes to death in Iceland, what is most striking about the country

is its totally unspoilt environment, conserved despite the major economic development of recent decades which has not here been accompanied by the mistakes typical of industrialised societies. The main sources of income are still the more traditional activities, such as fishing, fish processing, stockbreeding and agriculture, based mainly on pasture - not polluting either. Icelanders make incredible efforts to safeguard their natural heritage, even for minor matters.

There is a revealing anecdote on this subject. When, some years ago, the practice of baling hay in sturdy protective cellophane - as seen in fields all over Europe - was widely introduced, many thought that, although it meant the fodder would no longer rot, all those white cylinders scattered across Iceland's lovely meadows were a true eyesore. The matter developed into a national issue and, not long afterwards, the German manufacturer was asked to change the colour of the packaging from white to green, decidedly less noticeable. Such attention to environmental policy coupled with the fact that the country's primary energy sources are of geothermal and hydroelectric origin - hence free from harmful emissions - and a population density similar to that of the Sahara, make it easy to understand why Iceland, about to enter the third millennium, has remained practically unchanged since the times when the Vikings wiped out the forests. Before 874, the year in which a few valiant Norwegians landed, the island was at least partially covered with huge birch woods, as revealed by the sagas and other historical records. Man's activities, the cooling climate, natural catastrophes and the erosion of fertile terrain caused by over-sized flocks have reduced the primitive forests to a hundredth of the whole. Of this, less than just a quarter is farmland, pasture and terrain blanketed with musk and lichen; one tenth is covered with glaciers and all the rest is a boundless desert stretching from one horizon to the other, pockmarked with masses of lava that have been corroded by rivers and glaciers, traversed by strange undulations and rows of rounded cones in unlikely colours, scattered with fields of lava solidified in wrinkles and shattered crusts, given an even more alien appearance by expanses of cinders and pumice from which rise surreal petrified figures. Raging rivers, often confined within deep basaltic gorges, descend from the huge ice-caps, their waters clouded by the tons of sediment transported down to the valley. It is not in the least surprising that, in the Sixties, the Apollo astronauts prepared for their lunar landing in these severe spaces, so alien to man.

As every Icelander can confirm, this absolute and magnificent solitude creates such a sensitivity towards rare life forms, colours and light that a personal inner fantasy world tends to prevail over the physical reality. Beneath the unpredictable skies of Sprengisandur or Thorsmörk, along the northern fjords, on the banks of the crater-lake Viti or Myvatn - which alone justifies a trip to Iceland - it becomes easy to understand why a sense of magic is innate to the obstinate and proud people who live on this island hovering between the real world and the realms of the imagination. At the foot of the thundering Skógafoss falls, it is therefore only natural to consider the rainbow that has just materialised before you a bridge between sky and land, built with fire to prevent the frost giants from reaching the home of the gods, Valhalla. One evening, at Höfn, I was lucky enough to hear stories old and new of elves and sorcery; I learned why at a certain spot the road makes an improbable detour around a hill, believed to be the centuries-old home of a good spirit; I heard tales of souls returned among mortals for a last farewell. The hours passed quietly and, outside the window, the sky turned to burning gold, then fire and indigo striped with pink, without darkness ever getting the upper hand. On that strange arctic night, nothing I heard sounded incredible or even ridiculous. Magic is an ancient heritage of the Icelandic people, nor could it be otherwise, but it is lived inwardly, with reserve and pride, never openly manifested. It is the intimate, reassuring knowledge that they can "feel" their land and live in harmony with it and

the vibrant energy that runs through it: an ability lost by all those societies that, for the over-abused sake of progress, have given up their souls for a virtual, plastic and terribly artificial world.

Iceland is different. Crossing the immensity of this island is like plunging into mysterious passages, into the forgotten and unexplored depths that still exist inside us.

Signs of amazing occurrences can be seen in the now-shattered lava of Lakagígar, in which only musk, lichen and a few obstinate herbs grow. In the relatively young volcanic areas such as those around Landmannallaugar or Laki, the landscape is unreal, still, luminous, made of contrasting colours brought together to fantastic effect. It stirs visions of the long-gone times when the world was divided in its primeval elements, struggling towards a definitive form. On the black beaches within sight of the basaltic headland of Dyrhólaey, amidst the blocks of solidified lava of Dimmuborgir - the convoluted "black castles" that rise for miles on the banks of Lake Myvatn - against the background of the great mound of Hverfell or in the Asbyrgi canyon (according to legend a hoofprint left by Odinn's horse) such thoughts are aided by the ratio of the country's surface area (more than 38,000 square miles) and its population (230,000 inhabitants, most of which concentrated in Reykjavík and Akureyri). As all the towns are in the coastal areas, in many parts of the island man seems an accessory, a secondary element. Almost everywhere, from the Alps to the Himalayas, from the Andean valleys to the great expanses of Alaska, the natural environment has over the centuries been tampered with to some degree; even in the remotest parts of the planet you will often come across a track for vehicles or the signs of human settlement, however primitive. In Iceland you can hike for days without seeing trace of man while the comparison with amazing natural architecture is constant. The interior of the island, in particular, is a practically uncontaminated environment, a timeless world still partially unexplored, which can be visited only during the summer months. The wind, a constant presence in the Icelandic skies, sings its sometimes gentle, sometimes raging song and the shadows cast by the clouds playfully increase the confusion of eyes already stunned by the rapid succession of unreal forms and images. The landscape assumes a mythical dimension. Dragons with huge angular bodies crouch amidst the

22 top *The small church of Thingvellir is one of the most famous national monuments in Iceland and stands in the middle of a vast volcanic area situated 30 miles from Reykjavik; it is here that the republic was declared in 1944. This site is all the more sacrosanct because for nearly a thousand years - from 930 onwards - the Althing, the first parliament in the world, met here in the open air.*

22 bottom *Only the extreme northern tip of the mainland comes close to the Arctic circle but this is enough to mean that, in summer, Icelandic nights can no longer be considered such. In June the sight of the midnight sun in the north of the country is always a thrilling experience, weather permitting, of course.*

23 top *Although situated in the very centre of the capital, the Tjörn (which means "the lake") is a much-appreciated natural habitat for a considerable number of bird species.*

23 bottom *Practically all the Icelandic rivers are of glacial origin; born of countless smaller streams come together, near the sea they often run on the bottom of wide alluvial plains made of dissolved materials, such that the bed is a myriad of curves. In similar environments orientation becomes truly arduous and this is partly why the inhabitants of the island always recommend the utmost caution to adventurous trekkers. Iceland is a country that must be understood, loved and, most of all, respected.*

rocks, faces of millenary creatures beckon from the shapeless masses of solidified lava, imperceptible movements leave fleeting impressions on the retina and trouble overexcited souls. But the apprehension vanishes instantly with the appearance of a tenacious patch of green. Soft cushions of musk growing on the edge of a crystal-clear spring, small shocking pink flowers popping up almost miraculously between one stone and another and twisted trees taking root behind a boulder return you to a familiar earthly dimension, the world around you. This resolute will to live is yet another reminder that, despite the abstract scenery and metaphysical silences, Iceland is a part of this world, however unusual it may look. And however strange this may seem, it is a land inhabited by people of this world, totally unlike those taciturn characters mentioned a few pages earlier. Despite their geographical isolation, the people of Iceland are dynamic, bright, and determined, looking to the future. They are the world's leading users of the Internet, the percentage of software owned per capita gives them a rightful place in the firmament of Homo tecnologicus, they are among the most assiduous readers on the planet and, it goes without saying, among the most cultured. The young people are hyperactive, attentive to international cultural ferment and so creative that in just a few years they have given world rock such names as the Sugarcubes, Björk and GusGus, whose post-punk music conceals the north European soul of twilight explorers.

The Icelanders are a model of democracy and political equilibrium; in this country - which has no army - women have gained an equality of rights and social importance still considered utopian elsewhere. In recent times, the president of the Republic and the mayor of Reykjavík have been. The capital - the northernmost in the world - is a modern city in the true sense of the word: full of green areas, totally devoid of industrial waste, heated by boiling water from the nearby geothermal springs and run on electricity produced by the hydroelectric plants; a good 90 per cent of its buildings were constructed after the Second World War. A miniature metropolis, the symbol of national prosperity, it is in constant and rapid evolution, full of life, ambitious, vivacious, colourful and prone to sudden changes in fashion. The streets of the city centre are

24-25 Jökulsárlón is one of the main tourist attractions on the south-east coast; in the summer months small cruises can even be made on boats steered by true experts of navigation in difficult waters. To maintain the routes free at all times and the icebergs away from the jetty, rubber dinghies work, like sheepdogs with their flocks, to drive back the masses of ice.

26-27 The very architecture of Reykjavík shows that Iceland is still a man-sized country.

28-29 Hvítárvatn is a large lake formed of water from the melted Langjökull glacier, on the central highland.

30-31 The Icelandic horse is an integral part of the island's typical landscape.

constantly filled with heavy traffic, an apparent paradox when you shift your gaze to the splendid mountains - strictly devoid of all signs of civilisation - that surround the city. The shop windows, restaurants and boutiques do not even hint at the compulsory solitude suffered by the island in the first decades of the 20th century. Characterised by a very good lifestyle and a functional architecture that is truly man-size, Reykjavík houses all the government and administration institutions, the head offices of the country's main communications systems, numerous manufacturing and food industries, as well as sports amenities and swimming pools, schools and university, libraries and museums (an extremely interesting one is dedicated to Ásmundar Sveinsson and the Thjódhminjasafn Íslands, exhibiting records of the Viking era), cinemas, theatres and orchestras. The city's cultural scenario is utterly frenetic and its fifty or so publishers manage to replenish almost as many bookshops on a regular basis. In addition, five newspapers have altogether a circulation of 100,000 copies a day - an astonishing achievement to be sure! It is equally surprising that in the face of the evident and rapid expansion of fashions imported from the rest of Europe and America via the most popular mass-media, the inhabitants of Reykjavík - and the whole island in general - have managed to conserve and develop the nation's rich cultural heritage. The tongue of the Vikings, who started to colonise the island in the 9th century, has remained unchanged since then and this has permitted a remarkable continuity between past and present, kept alive not only by the reading of mediaeval literature but also thanks to the conservation of original place names, often bound to some episode narrated in the ancient sagas and Skaldic poems. Although this country did not gain independence from the Danish crown until 1944, it is the home of the oldest parliament in the world, the Althing, established in 930 at Pingvellir, and is perhaps the only nation to have succeeded in passing on to its descendants the vicissitudes of a people from their very first day in a new land in written records. It is thrilling to know that any young Icelander dressed in blue jeans and T-shirt can read the entire history of his/her nation in the original language without difficulty while elsewhere this requires adequate and lengthy preparation. To safeguard this heritage, which is

rooted in the conscience of each and every Icelander, the adoption of all neologisms or words of foreign origin in the spoken language has been strictly avoided; words already in use are adapted to new meanings or a suitable periphrasis is devised for every modern need, hence the telephone is known simply the "simi", (the wire along which the communication travels). Despite this, practically all the population is bilingual (correct English is spoken by nearly everyone, both in the capital and in the remotest villages) and many speak other languages. This modern approach is a striking contrast with the primeval appearance of much of the territory. This is one of the most active volcanic lands in the world, where the forces of nature act fast, giving rise to changing geological situations witnessed nowhere else on earth. This is due to the fact that Iceland was produced by the drifting European and American continents; situated right on the Mid-Atlantic Ridge, it is still subject to the turbulent tectonic processes that formed it and that are now breaking it in two at a speed of just under an inch per year. This is why the island boasts a remarkable number of natural phenomena that make it truly unique: geysers, fumaroles, mudpots, lava flows that have solidified in the strangest shapes, solfataras, thermal rivers and lakes are all the result of the volcanism that led to its formation and that knows no respite. Down in its innermost depths lurk constant tensions, lacerations, hidden forces that explain the frequent eruptions, the telluric motions and the even more bizarre phenomena that the inhabitants of this strange corner of the world are always happy to narrate. I remember the tale of a lake near Húsavík, on the northern coast, that one fine day was covered with a dense and increasingly warm mist, until the waters started to boil, offering speechless onlookers a miraculous catch of thousands of fish boiled to perfection. Or again, the strange adventure experienced by a family of peasants - once more in the Húsavík area - awoken one night by a horrendous roar, accompanied by jolts and jerks that seemed to be trying to demolish their humble home in one fell swoop. When all became suddenly quiet, the farmer went outside to explore the farm and came back, reassuring his wife as to the effect of the earthquake with a few, concise words: "Nothing serious, everything is still standing. But tomorrow I'll have to build a bridge over to the tool shed.

Let's go back to bed". Quite simply, a huge fissure had opened in the ground a few yards from their bedroom. They say the farm is still there, with its bridge and the shed on the other side: it will take some years yet to fill the chasm. If these seem incredible stories you only have to go to Reykjahlíd where an old church is half-buried in the lava that flowed down in the 18th century during the Krafla volcano eruption, passing without destroying it. Familiarity with similar freaks of nature has become a part of the Icelandic character since when, more than eleven centuries ago, Ingólfur Arnarson landed in the bay of Reykjavík and built his house there. Iceland is a living land, a constantly changing universe, with a history marked by the cyclical repetition of tremors and eruptions. The most frightening occurred in 1783, when the ground near Lakagígar opened in a 18-mile-long fissure and for days and days the gaping chasm spewed incandescent magma and toxic gases: the sky was darkened for six months and the haze poisoned the meadows causing a famine of huge proportions that led to the death of hundreds of people and much of the livestock.

For a long time the rest of Europe thought that Iceland was the antechamber to hell. Times have changed, the seismologists can predict the most dangerous cataclysms fairly well in advance now, but the Icelanders are still as proud and obstinate as ever. The cities may be destroyed by eruptions but they rebuild them the same or even more beautiful, right on top of those lost. The last time this happened was in 1973, on the island of Heimaey, when more than five thousand inhabitants were evacuated in just a few hours with impressive efficiency and not a single victim. Perhaps it will happen again, and yet again the Icelanders will set to work without submission, just as every day without fail they continue to plant new trees to make the whole island green once more. I understand such love and determination because Iceland is a splendid, wild country fashioned by wind, water, ice and fire that pours from the depths of the earth; it is made of fuming mountains, rocks that rise to form breath-taking arches, it is harsh outflows of lava and gentle meadows that slope down to the sea. Iceland will capture your soul, almost before you realise it, and will not return it all - a small piece will remain there, amidst volcanoes and ice, for ever.

Nature becomes spectacle

32 top *The climate of the vast central highland is much harsher than that of the coastal strip and this area remains snow-clad until late spring. The picture shows the glacial valley of the Tungnaa river, near Landmannalaugar and clearly the dirt track that passes not far from here can be used only in the summer months. This is a true misfortune for the Icelandic people because this awkward communication route offers the advantage of halving the distance between Reykjavík and Akureyri, the country's two major cities.*

32 bottom *Seen from the open sea, the coast near Höfn is dominated by the vast Vatnajökull ice-cap. Extending over 3,229 square miles, equal to 11 per cent of the island's entire surface area, this ice giant culminates at the 6,950 feet of Hvannadalshnjúkur, the highest peak in Iceland.*

33 *Skágafoss is perhaps the most attractive waterfall in Iceland, or at least it can contend this title with Gullfoss; in just one straight, impressive leap of 196 feet, the water coming from the Myrdalsjökull glacier thunders down from the basaltic bastion that surrounds the coast here a few hundred yards from the sea. Situated along the Ring Road, not far from Vík, this natural attraction delights tourists who can venture just a few yards from the mighty wall of water.*

34-35 *During the rainy summer, musk grows on the bare lava fields that cover vast areas of the island, turning them bright green.*

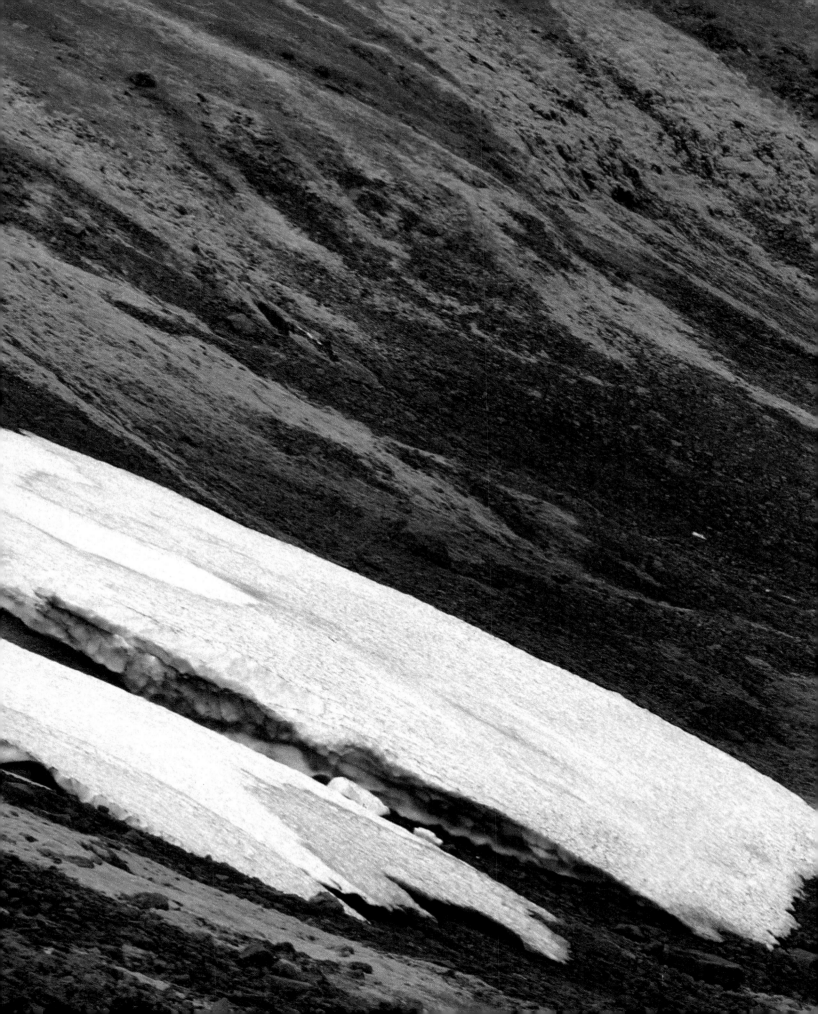

Life tinged with green

36 left *The volcanic origin of the Icelandic territory gives rise to totally unique and bizarre phenomena, as is the case of the delightful Hraunfossar falls in the west of the island. This remarkable work of nature is generated by the rain and glacial waters that are absorbed by the porous terrain a few miles farther up; they then run underground on an impermeable layer until they come to a deep fracture through which they flow out onto the surface.*

36 right *The plain that extends around Hvítarvatn is full of marshy areas which, with the first rays of summer sun, develop a thick, grassy vegetation, creating a favourite habitat for geese and wild duck. Despite its harsh appearance, Iceland is full of similar miracles.*

37 *Inland, where the climate is more severe, musk is the most common form of vegetation. Capable of surviving the terrible rigours of winter, with the first warm days it turns the dull lava fields bright green and grows to form what look like strange velvet cushions. It is thanks to the humble but tenacious Bryophyta that even the sweeping lunar-like area of Landmanallaugar manages to appear slightly less hostile in summer.*

Vertical water

38-39 It is a cliché that Iceland is a land of ice and fire; this is absolutely true but a more complete picture would include water, or rather waterfalls. It can be said without hesitation that this is the land of waterfalls. The rivers are usually quite short and the topography of the island means that there are no great differences in ground levels. The water does not therefore fall from dizzy heights but the quantity and flow are amazing. Supplied by the great glaciers of the interior, hundreds of rivers run down to the sea all along Iceland's perimeter, picking up countless tributaries along the way and quickly turning into roaring masses of extraordinary intensity. Godafoss is the most easily-accessible waterfall, close to the main road and not far from Akureyri.

39 top Far more impressive is Dettifoss, supplied by the raging Jökulsa á Fjollum, that runs in the north of the country; 203 feet high, this is considered the most powerful waterfall in Europe. It formed after a telluric tremor which deviated the course of the river towards a deep fissure in the basaltic plain; its forceful impact is digging the ravine below at the rate of some inches per year.

39 bottom The name Godafoss means literally "waterfall of the gods" and according to tradition it is here that the Vikings, converted to Christianity, threw away their statues of pagan gods. Another legend tells that the Icelanders used to worship the holy trinity of Odinn, Thor and Freyr in the three main streams.

A surreal and splendid world

40-41 *Geologically speaking, Iceland is the youngest country in Europe; the forces of nature have had not a moment's respite since the island emerged from the cold waters of the northern Atlantic, driven by a volcanic fury still active today. Proof of this vitality lies in the numerous geothermal springs that gush forth in various parts of the country, often restrained and exploited to produce electricity or to heat greenhouses and homes. The area of Geysir, roughly 60 miles from Reykjavik, is so famous that it has given its name to all the warm water springs in the world. Today the Great Geysir is tired and its jet has become a rare spectacle but not far away is Strokkur which now thrills visitors. Every five minutes or so this highly energetic geyser spouts a column of boiling water and steam 60 feet high into the air.*

41 top *The entire area around Geysir is marked by extraordinary natural phenomena: these two warm springs, known as Blesi, boast very different colours despite being so close. The turquoise hues of the one to the fore are produced by the colloidal silica content of the water.*

41 centre *Far more inaccessible than Geysir is the thermal site of Hveravellir, in the heart of the central highlands. Here the attractive pool known as Bláhver, or Blue spring, is surrounded by banks of silica concretion.*

41 bottom *The deep pools of hot water at Hveravellir reach a temperature of almost 244 F and lie in the middle of the central highland.*

42-43 *One of the most picturesque waterfalls in Iceland, Seljalanfoss deserves a special mention: plunging as if from a diving board on a high basaltic cliff, its waters tumble down in an elegant 130-foot arch. This spectacle can be admired in southern Iceland along the Ring Road, the island's main means of communication. A path traced at its base of the falls allows visitors to pass behind its foaming jet of water. There is no risk but a thrill is guaranteed.*

44 *Because of its surreal landscapes, of truly alien fascination, Landmannalaugar is one of the most famous sites on the island.*
In summer the deeply eroded sides of the uneven hills cover briefly with grass and lichen, offering a spectacle of primeval beauty. However incredible it may seem, a whole network of paths criss-cross this wild-looking region and long hikes can be made, stopping to spend the night in refuge huts situated a day's march from each other.

45 *Although its idyllic appearance would suggest otherwise, Thingvellir is another area of intense tectonic activity. This vast lava plain, covered with lovely vegetation is, in actual fact, the point at which the two halves of the island, corresponding to the European and the American plates, are separating. This is demonstrated by the numerous deep fissures that cross it from one end to the other. This location, steeped in history, is where in 1974 the nation celebrated the 1100th anniversary of the first permanent settlement on Icelandic soil.*

46 Particularly active from
a geothermal point of view, the region
of Landmannalaugar - situated in the
south of the country - is quite famous but,
in a land where hot springs, fumaroles
and geysers are considered perfectly
normal, this would not suffice to explain
such celebrity. Actually, the display
of colour sported here by nature
is breath-taking. This is the domain
of rhyolite, an eruptive rock that comes in
an extraordinary variety of shades - from
ochre to orange, brown to plum, yellow to
pale green. No landscape painter would
dare contrive such combinations.

47 A perpetually smoking solfatara
is active at the foot of Brennisteinsalda,
the multicoloured mountain that is one
of the major attractions of
Landmannalaugar. The tooth of dark
rock visible to the left, close to the summit,
is a columnar basaltic outcrop,
a reminder of intense effusive activity.

48-49 In late spring, the
Landmannalaugar landscape is
dominated by the pastel shades of rhyolite
and white snow-fields not yet melted.
However fascinating, this territory
is extremely hostile towards man; usually
a visit to the internal regions of the island
calls for physical fitness, a love of
adventure and of wide, open and silent
spaces as well as careful planning.
Proper clothing, sleeping bags, tents and
plenty of supplies are absolutely essential
because only a few huts will be
encountered, even along the main trails,
and provisions are hard if not impossible
to come by. Such dedication will, however,
be rewarded by a journey through
a wilderness unequalled anywhere else
on earth.

50-51 *The geothermal area of Landmannalaugar has a truly unreal appearance; in these surroundings not a lot of imagination is needed to gain the sensation of having just landed on the uneven surface of Venus or Mars. Nevertheless, just half an hour's walk leads back to civilisation with a cosy refuge hut and camping site on the plain that opens at the base of the lava flow, visible in the background. This delightful region may be remote and only accessible with 4WD vehicles, but in summer it is a favourite destination of nature-lovers who, after a hard day's hike, relax in the waters of a famous warm spring.*

51 top *Near Krísuvík, on the Reykanes peninsula is the most powerful outflow of underground vapours in the world. The area is surrounded by solfataras and boiling mudpots which give the landscape - heavy with the unmistakable smell of sulphur - a Dantesque atmosphere. The terrain is boiling hot and visits call for caution.*

Iceland, a daughter of the sea

52 top *On the southern coast, close to the town of Vík, stand the high cliffs of Dyrhólaey. The top of this formidable basaltic balcony affords a sweeping view over black volcanic beaches.*

52 centre *The waves of the Atlantic break violently on the characteristic black sand of Vík, eternally fashioning new forms.*

52 bottom *A lovely view of the Vestmannaeyjar islands, rising off the southern coast. The only settlement on the small archipelago, Heimaey, was totally evacuated in 1973 when it was semi-submerged by the mighty lava flow that gushed forth from a volcano that appeared literally before the astonished eyes of the population. When the fury of the phenomenon had subsided, thanks partly to the men who bombarded the front of burning lava for days on end with sea water, the districts destroyed were promptly rebuilt and today life is very active here, especially thanks to its modern port facilities. Another singular local feature is the small island of Surtsey, which emerged from the Ocean in 1963 following an underwater eruption; it is a copy on a reduced scale of Iceland, a daughter of the sea.*

53 *The Westmannaeyjar islands are also famous for the large numbers of birds that have colonised the rugged coasts. Note the surreal presence of an authentic road sign fixed to the rock - remarkable proof that maritime traffic is really intense in these parts.*

Fantastic natural architecture

54 *The Skaftafell National Park is justly proud of the Svartifoss waterfall, in the south-east part of the island. The name means "Black waterfall" and it boasts an unequalled natural setting, surrounded as it is by a curtain of organ-pipe basaltic columns. These remarkable formations are the result of the slow cooling of a particular type of lava and are to be seen in numerous other parts of the island.*

54-55 *The Hvitifoss waterfall is situated near Kirkjubæjarklaustur, a small but important village on the Ring Road in the south of the country. The surrounding region of Skaftá is famous for its beautiful scenery, deeply furrowed by the course of the numerous rivers that descend from the nearby Myrdalsjökull and Vatnajökull glaciers. As can easily be seen in this picture, Iceland is the ideal destination for those wishing to make a trek in close contact with nature, far from all signs of civilisation. The boundless expanses of the inland areas should not however be tackled lightly, because in these parts the term "desert" is used literally.*

The ice giant

56 top left *Also known as the "Gem of Iceland", Lake Jökulsárlón is perpetually littered with icebergs; these form because when the front of the glacier enters the water it is subjected to such a thrust upwards that it breaks into large blocks.*

56 top right *Depending on the point it is viewed from, Vatnajökull offers very different sceneries, with numerous minor glaciers descending from it, especially to the south.*

56 bottom *Clearly visible from above are the seracs and morainic detritus transported down to the valley by Breidamerkurjökull, a branch of the larger Vatnajökull.*

56-57 *Vatnojökull is one of the largest glaciers in the world and not just in extension: at many points it is more than 3,000 feet thick.*

58-59 *Although seemingly impossible, the Vatnajökull ice-cap conceals active volcanoes.*

60-61 *In 1996 the media of the whole world helped to make Iceland known during the spectacular sub-glacial eruption of Vatnajökull, which started on 29th September and ended in the month of November. The molten rock (magma) spewed out from the mouth of the volcano, calculated as more than 500 million cubic metres, caused the sudden melting of half a cubic mile of ice, creating an unreal landscape on the surface. The huge mass of water produced flowed south at a rate of approximately 44 thousand cubic metres per second, fortunately in a practically uninhabited area. The wave bore with it huge blocks of ice and enormous quantities of mud destroying a long stretch of the main road; in just a few weeks the Icelanders had restored the links.*

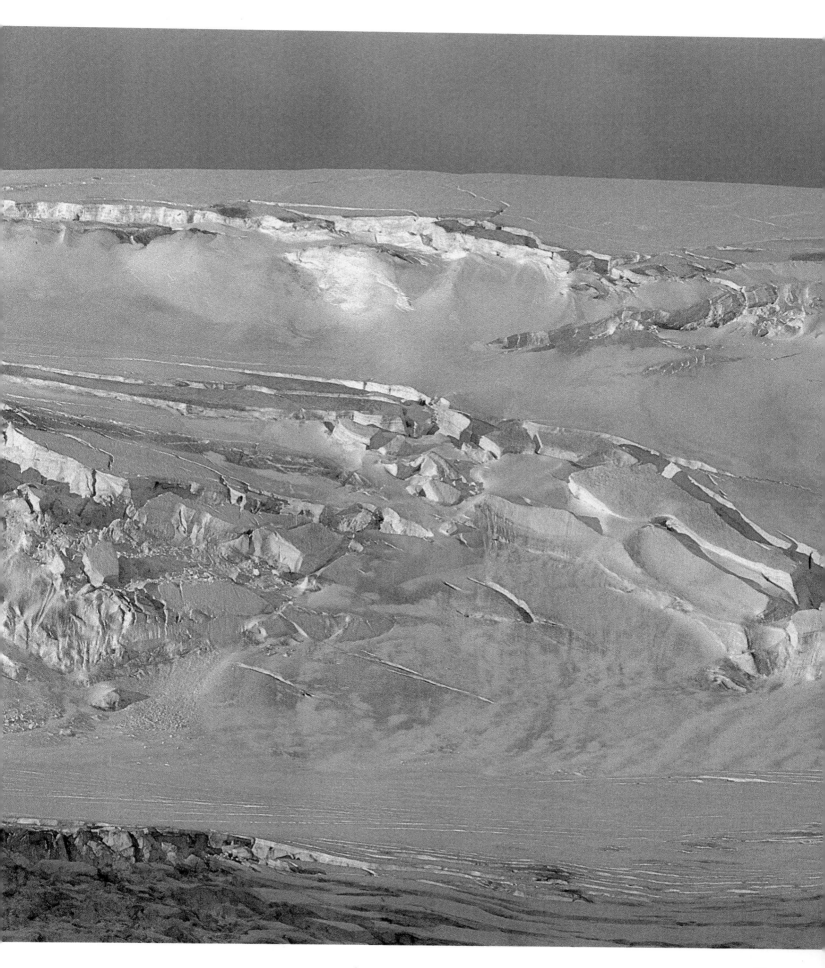

Ice and more ice

62 top *The picture shows the peak and crater on the summit of Hekla, Iceland's biggest volcano. Situated in the south of the island, it is 4,890 feet high and nearly always enveloped in vapour and cloud, hence its menacing name: "the hooded". This ice giant is famous for its frequent and violent eruptions.*

62 bottom *With its 285 square miles Myrdalsjökull is the fourth largest glacier in Iceland. The south-eastern part of the ice-cap conceals an active volcano, Katla, which is known to have erupted 20 times, the last having been in 1918. Sub-glacial eruptions, common also to Vatnajökull, melt huge quantities of ice and the wave that emerges from the slopes of the glacier - known as* hlaup *- develops a frightening destructive force. In some cases the flow of the mass of water has equalled the of the maximum one of the Amazon river: 7 million cubic feet per second.*

62-63 *The photograph shows one of the impressive terminal tongues of Eyjafallajökull, the fifth largest glacier on the island.*
Iceland is the land of ice-caps par excellence, 11 per cent of its territory being perpetually covered with ice. This has over the geological ages shaped the huge expanses of lava, carving deep fjords that indent the coasts and give the mountains their characteristic rugged appearance.

64-65 *Near the large glaciers the climate is quite severe even in summer, as shown by the presence of slabs of ice on the surface of Langisjör. This lake is set at the foot of Skaftárjökull, a branch of the far larger Vatnajökull.*

Primeval landscapes

66-67 *The Laxa river, approximately 31 miles long, is the only inlet and outlet of Lake Myvatn and famous for its trout and salmon, the largest found in Iceland. On the horizon, to the right, is the outline of mount Vindbeljarfall, at 1,738 feet one of the highest points in the region.*

67 top *The erratic contours of Lake Myvatn, in the north of the island, extend over a vast lava plain; in some parts small islets of brightly-coloured bizarre-shaped volcanic stone rise from the placid waters and have stimulated numerous legends. A recent survey revealed that the great majority of Icelanders believe in the existence of elves and other supernatural creatures. Although this may seem strange, anyone who has spent a few days alone in such places knows that in Iceland even the rocks, ice and moss have souls.*

67 centre *The not very poetically named Myvatn (which means "midge lake") is the fourth largest lake in Iceland. The beauty of this place and its abundance of fauna have driven the Icelandic authorities to declare the entire zone a National Protected Area. Situated near the spectacular Krafla fault and on the edge of the vast northern desert, the lake has become one of the most popular tourist destinations in the country.*

67 bottom *Hundreds of now-extinct eruptive cones, such as that of the Grabrok volcano, are dotted over the changing Icelandic landscape, an eternal reminder of a restless subsoil.*

A restless land

68 top *At one point the crater of the Askja volcano, situated in a highly inaccessible part of the central highland, filled with warm water to form a lake; Öskjuvatn, the deepest lake on the island, is visible in the background. It has been calculated that over the last 15,000 years, since the Ice Age ended, more than 200 volcanoes have been active in Iceland, of which 30 of them from the time of the first human settlement to the present day.*

68 bottom *These bubbling mudpots surrounded by sulphur concretion are situated at Hverarönd, just a few miles from Lake Myvatn. A volcanic land par excellence, Iceland is the largest emerging part of a long oceanic ridge; this flanks a fracture in the earth's crust through which is forced the molten rock that spreads the plates and separates the drifting continents. Iceland, together with the Azores, constitutes the most impressive piece of this fracture and is 99 per cent effusive, the rest being sediment. Strangely, one of the country's great resources is the pumice stone expelled from the volcanoes, used as building material and exported.*

68-69 Not far from Lake Myvatn, to the east, lie the Narmaskardi solfataras. This area has a surreal appearance, the terrain being dotted with holes that steam, fume and whistle deafeningly; there are also numerous bubbling mudpots, typical manifestations of secondary volcanism. These infernal cauldrons are supplied by surface water that filters into the ground and is heated by the molten rock below through deep fissures in the earth's crust. Such scenes, common in Iceland, take visitors' imagination back in time, to the very creation of the universe; paradoxically Iceland is a land which has been formed in very recent, geologically speaking, times.

69 right The Namaskardi area constitutes, without doubt, one of the most surreal scenarios on the island and is part of the Namafjall fissure, active proof of the Mid-Atlantic Ridge below, the opposing and contrasting forces of which tend to separate the two tectonic plates that form Iceland at a rate of a few millimetres per year.

70-71 The geothermal area of Krafla, situated a few miles from Lake Myvatn, beyond the Namafjall ridge, is at present one of the most active volcanic zones in the world. From 1975 on, a spectacular series of eruptions was marked by high lava fountains. These emissions of molten rock continued in close succession for the next 10 years, creating vast fields of lava and picturesque lakes then formed amidst the multicoloured rhyolite hills.

71 Krafla is a very unusual volcano, a huge caldera with its edges devastated by repeated eruptions. One of these, in 1725, produced an explosive crater which filled with meteoric water: the resulting lake is called Viti, which means "Hell".

72-73 In the Krafla area the white vapour rising behind one of the multicoloured folds is discharged by the local geothermal power station, built in 1973. This type of plant has the huge advantage of not generating harmful vapours or waste. Today, practically all Icelandic industry uses the energy produced by the hydroelectric stations and geothermal plants provide the heating for more than 90 per cent of the country's homes.

74-75 *The village of Siglufjördur is set in a sheltered position at the end of the fjord of the same name, in the north of the country. Once an important fishing centre and home of herring-processing plants, following the drastic reduction in the numbers of these fish in Icelandic waters, it suffered a long period of decline partially overcome in recent years thanks to tourism. The dramatic views offered by the fjords are true monuments to the extremes of nature witnessed in Iceland, where the land embraces the sea.*

Where the land embraces the sea

75 top *Extending into the Atlantic like a sort of open hand, the region of Westfjords is one of the least populated and most inhospitable of Iceland. This makes it the best place for those wishing to enter into symbiosis with untamed nature, made of differentiated scenarios, harsh and gentle in one. Isafjördur, the capital, stands on a tongue of land in the middle of the fjord of Isafjardardjúp and is the only real town, as well as the obligatory point of departure for visits to the area.*

75 centre *Many of the numerous Westfjords - this is Önundarfjördur - are now deserted, with few traces of the times when bold communities of fishermen lived here; coastal settlements that look close on the maps are often separated by imposing natural barriers made of mountain ranges or impassable cliffs.*

75 bottom *Mountains and rugged cliffs tower above a deep-blue sea making the fjords of the north a setting of uncommon beauty.*

76-77 *Incredibly isolated in the middle of the snow, a farm stands solitary, inland from Nordfjördur, just a few miles from the village of Neskaupstadur. This is in the Eastfjord region, perhaps that showing the most marked contrasts in this land of opposites that live together. Here too, every fjord boasts its own little town or cluster of villages, in each of which the fishing industry takes precedence over all else - save for the case of a few tenacious farmers who prefer to live in the wide open spaces; the plains that stretch out behind the coast are more fertile than would be expected and during spring-time the pastures become of an inpredictable luxuriant green.*

The splendid west

78-79 Búdir, of which the picture shows the church, was once a major fishing port on the Snæffelnes peninsula; today it is an isolated and silent spot where people come to enjoy the austere beauty of the surrounding region, perhaps one of the loveliest in western Iceland, thanks partly to its historical importance.

79 top left A stretch of the beach of Búdir is marked by the unusual colour of a certain type of lava.

79 top right The church of Helgafell, not far from Stykkishólmur, stands on the foundations of a 12th-century monastery. The nearby hill is said to have miraculous powers.

80-81 This farm is near Akranes, one of the main towns in western Iceland and one of the largest ports in the country. Given the isolation in which many Icelanders still live, it is no surprise that reading is one of the most common pastimes. The number of books published per capita every year in Iceland is the highest in the world.

Animals roaming free

82 top *Sheep-rearing is a little different in Iceland as the animals are left out to graze freely at the beginning of the warm season and are then rounded up in September during expeditions on horseback or in 4WD cars. Sheep and rams living almost wild have become an integral part of the scenery since they were first brought to the island by the Vikings.*

82 centre left *The puffin with its black and white plumage and delightful beak is one of the characteristic inhabitants of the Icelandic coasts.*

82 centre right *As Iceland has never been connected to either the European or the American continents, few animals are native to the island. Apparently the only indigenous land mammal is the Arctic fox, although this species probably came to the island on an iceberg before the arrival of the Viking settlers. All the other animals were imported by man, including the reindeer, brought from Scandinavia between 1771 and 1787, during a great famine. When the idea of transforming the Icelanders into nomad herdsmen failed, the animals turned wild and about 3,000 now live in the eastern valleys.*

82 bottom *Home to huge colonies of land, sea and marsh birds, both migratory and resident, Iceland attracts ornithologists and bird-watching enthusiasts from all over the world. It is not uncommon to see very rare species here, native to North America and unknown in the rest of Europe.*

83 *Puffins form large colonies on the high rocks of the island, such that the total number amounts to approximately 10 million. These comical birds - their scientific name is* Fratercula artica *- usually nest at the top of the cliffs, where the terrain allows them to dig the deep nests where the females lay their eggs. Being creatures of habit, the couples return every year at the end of May to the same hole as the previous season.*

84 top *Killer whales, unmistakable with their white and black back and characteristic large tail fin, can be sighted off the coasts and in the waters of the Vestmannaeyjar islands in particular.*

84 centre *Sperm whales are still quite common in the seas around Iceland although it has not yet adhered to the international suspension of whale-hunting.*

84 bottom *This humpback whale has been photographed during one of the spectacular leaps that make the species famous; as for the killer and sperm whales the best time to sight these large cetaceans is between late spring and the end of summer.*

84-85 *Numerous seal colonies populate the jagged coasts of the island; these congenial mammals can be seen all year round basking in the sun on black lava beaches or lying undisturbed on the ice. Iceland has two species: the common seal - seen in the picture - and the grey seal. The former is by far the more common, indeed roughly half of the entire world population is thought to live here.*

Like beads on a necklace

86 top *Iceland is a place of ferocious contrasts in scenery but also in climate. The coastal strip may enjoy the benefit brought by the warm Gulf Stream but the central highland is the undisputed domain of cold Arctic winds and looks like a barren and inhospitable desert. This has meant that since the times of the first settlements the Icelanders have been able to live only on a small portion of the territory, on the shores of that sea that has always been their main source of sustenance. The towns, small or large, are therefore distributed along the island's perimeter like beads on an enormous necklace, glimmering with the resolution of a proud and obstinate people. The picture shows Grenivík, a small town on the Eyjafjördur, in the north of the country.*

86 bottom *A typical town of the Eastfjords, Seydisfjördur has fewer than 1,000 inhabitants but until the early 20th century its population was a sixth of that of Reykjavík, making it the major town in the region. Of that golden era the town conserves numerous buildings which, added to the charming houses with multicoloured roofs, give it a typically Scandinavian appearance. Today, Seydisfjördur remains quite important because ferries from Europe arrive here.*

87 *As the home of the government, administrative, commercial and cultural capital, main centre for services, transport, communications and, in general, all other activities, Reykjavík is the heart and soul of today's Icelandic society. Despite this it has preserved a truly enviable human dimension, marked by large open spaces and attractive modern architecture.*

Reykjavík, a smogless capital

88 top *Until the early 20th century, Reykjavík was little more than a large village and only the rapid evolution of Icelandic society, today one of the most advanced in the western world, turned it into a modern city. This is why the capital boasts few monuments from the past and generally speaking the oldest buildings date only from the 18th century. Some of the most typical old houses - such as those seen here in the picture - are found in the area between the old harbour and the Tjörnin.*

88 centre *An example of Reykjavík's modernity is the fact that the Hallgrímskirkja, the large church that towers above the city's skyline dates from just 1970. The highest structure in the capital, its bell tower is considered the best place to enjoy a sweeping view of the town.*

88 bottom *Artistic activities and events are an important part of life in the capital, which plays a fundamental cultural role for these dynamic people. Reykjavík has numerous museums among which is the highly original construction of the Asmundur Sveinsson Museum, dedicated to the great artist who died in 1982.*

88-89 *Reykjavik has been the heart of the country since the first settler, Ingólfur Arnarson, decided in 874 to settle on the banks of the small lake that is today at the centre of the city. Ingólfur called the newly-born city "smoky bay" - this is what the name of the capital means - after the white clouds of steam he saw rising from* the ground, produced of course by the thermal springs; thanks to these natural phenomena, today Reykjavík can call itself a smokeless - and therefore a smogless - city. Every home is heated using the geothermal resources which produce the energy required by its inhabitants, and the air breathed here is almost totally pollution-free.

90-91 *Since it started to grow from the small village to a modern metropolis in the first decades of the 20th century, Reykjavík has expanded constantly. With more than 100,000 inhabitants the capital houses more than two-fifths of the population of the entire country and is the symbol of Iceland's rapid passage from rural society to modern technology.*

Akureyri, the capital of the north

92 top *Akureyri - the picture shows the main thoroughfare, Hafnarstraeti - is the most important city in the north as well as being the second most densely-populated in Iceland. Grown frenetically in this century thanks to its port, today it has 15,000 inhabitants, a highly respectable number considering that just 200 people lived here when it was raised to the status of municipality in 1862.*

92 bottom *Set in a splendid position on the fjord, a few miles from Akureyri, the Laufás farm includes a church and some turf buildings dating from the middle of the 19th century; once the residence of a well-to-do vicar, today it is a folklore museum. Because of numerous earthquakes, floods, perishable materials and the poverty in which Iceland was forced to live until the early 20th century, few truly ancient monuments have survived to the present day. This shortage is made up by the sagas, chronicles containing minute descriptions of historical events on the island starting from the Viking settlement.*

92-93 *Founded in a sheltered position at the end of the long Eyjfjördur, 37 miles from the open sea, today Akureyri is a modern-looking and bustling city. Blessed by a fairly mild climate despite its proximity to the Arctic circle, the fish industry makes it prosper and it has a university, a botanic garden and several museums. By local standards it can be deemed a true metropolis - a paradox typical of a nation where the common yardsticks are very relative and a major administrative and economic centre may have fewer than 2,000 inhabitants.*

Man's tenacious presence

94 top left *Djópivogur is a small village on the eastern coast, nearly entirely given over to fishing, despite being at the centre of a fairly fertile region with many farms. Historical sources tell that this area flourished in the 17th century as a trading centre, but the oldest buildings date from the times of the Danish merchants who controlled the local economy between 1788 and 1920.*

94 bottom left *Standing on the high basaltic headland of Dyrhólaey is the white silhouette of a lighthouse. Despite the introduction of modern technology some solitary spirits still live in many of the 60 and more luminous sentinels that watch over the coasts of Iceland. The inhabitants of this island are accustomed to total silence and boundless horizons: Iceland is the least densely-populated nation of the European continent.*

94 top right *Famous for the midnight sun and temperate summers, the northern fjords - the picture shows Eyjafjördur - are also known for their incredibly beautiful scenery which in winter becomes pure magic. The villages along the coasts deserve a visit not only for their bucolic atmosphere, they are also strategic points of departure for exploration of the surrounding wilderness.*

95 *A lone lighthouse stands on the extreme north-western tip of Reykjanes peninsula, the first region in south-west Iceland seen by visitors coming to the island by air. The bright colours are well-suited to the purpose of the structure but are also common to many buildings dotted all over the country - almost as if to accentuate their presence in a nature so immense as at times to become frightening.*

Well-being comes from the sea

96 top left *Canoes are left to dry at the Akureyri boat club. The Icelanders have close bonds with the sea which is a source of sustenance and pleasure, of life and death, of joy and pain. These people's lifestyle - so different from that of the rest of Europe for their deep and even mystical relationship with the surrounding environment - is the reflection of a looming, omnipresent nature, which often gives but sometimes destroys.*

96 top right *Seydisfjördur has a small but active fishing fleet; the soul of the Icelandic fishing industry is made of small villages scattered along the coasts of the island where the life of the entire population rotates around fishing and the processing on land of the catch. In these tiny communities, where everyone knows everyone else, there is little to think about except the boats, nets, the processing plants and, of course, the weather conditions.*

96 bottom *Olafsvík is the main port on the Snæffelsnes peninsula, in the west of the island. Renowned for its fishing fleet and the related activities of fish processing and conservation, the town is known to hikers as the point of departure for climbs to the top of Snæffelsjökull, the glacier with an ice-cap over the mouth of an extinct volcano. Jules Verne set the start of the famous descent in his "A Journey to the Centre of the Earth" here.*

96-97 *The fishing and processing industry covers almost 80 per cent of the country's exports. Crucial factors that make Icelandic fish highly appreciated on the international markets are the advanced techniques of freezing developed, the high standards of hygiene in the factories and absolutely reliable supplies.*

Settling means building

98 top *The architecture of Húsavík, the main town in the north-east and a well-equipped port, is a mark of considerable prosperity.*

98 bottom *This is the lighthouse of Stykkishólmur, the main town on the Snæffelsnes peninsula; the ferries arriving from the Westfjords dock in its efficient port after stopping at the island of Flatey.*

99 top *Today almost totally superseded, corrugated metal sheet was for a long time one of the most commonly-used materials for the construction of houses because it was strong and cheap. Timber, in fact, used to be quite a costly material and therefore was usually replaced with turf or metal sheet. At Seydisfjördur there is still a great number of houses built in old style and painted red with a particular anti-rust paint.*

100-101 *The town of Heimaey is seen here from the top of the not yet completely cooled lava flow that, in 1973, almost wiped out the town and its port facilities. The eruption started on 25th January when suddenly 40 or more columns of fire rose from a huge fissure; fortunately all the inhabitants managed to save themselves in the sea. Once more a flourishing port, Heimaey is today a symbol of Icelandic determination.*

The heritage of the past

102 *This traditional old Icelandic house is near Grindavík on the Reykjanes peninsula. The building is positioned to offer the minimum resistance to the prevailing winds in the area and is reinforced by two stone and turf walls. Houses such as this have special historical value for Icelanders because they represent a strong link with the past and are the memory of a rural society that started to disappear rapidly in the Forties.*

103 top left *The church of Vidmyrkirkjia dates from the 18th century and is therefore one of the oldest monuments in the country. The practically total absence of historical buildings in Iceland should be no surprise, just consider the shortage of timber following the destruction of many of the forests by the first settlers and the countless tremors that have, over the centuries, razed entire villages to the ground. Turf walls provide good insulation and are typical of ancient local architecture.*

103 top right *Close to the village of Skógar, in the south of the island, stands the most popular Icelandic folklore museum. Besides the outstanding collection of finds and former everyday objects, this important cultural institution is of interest because various types of dwelling used by the Icelanders over the centuries have been reconstructed here. As can be seen, roofs used to be covered with pieces of turf to increase the thermal insulation.*

103 bottom *Another folklore museum can be visited near Bolungarvík, a town of the Westfjords; this too has buildings reconstructed as in times past. A peculiar feature of the ancient building methods was the thickness of the dry walls, the inter-spacing being filled with turf and clay. This served to protect the structure against the force of the elements and to limit the loss of heat to a minimum.*

The children of Vikings

104 top *Extremely democratic people, Icelanders are very open-minded and reveal a strong sense of tolerance. This is why it is not uncommon in Reykjavík to see unusual groups of demonstrators in front of Parliament.*

104 bottom *In the 9th century AD the first Icelanders founded not just a nation but a form of republican government that was unique at the time. However, in 1264 Iceland was annexed to the Norwegian crown and then, in 1397, became a Danish colony. Full independence was not regained until 1944, approved by a plebiscite vote of 99.7 per cent.*
Every year, on 17th June, Independence Day is celebrated with general enthusiasm in the capital and in every other village and town in the country. A strong sense of national identity has been inherited by every Icelander as they have always had to face hardships that would have been unsurpassable had they not learnt to work together.

105 *Icelanders, for the most part urbanised and consciously cosmopolitan in their lifestyle and behaviour, have an innate passion for their land and for hiking. In a country where the forces of nature have such freedom of action, the views are without equal. The vast open spaces here offer opportunities that would be inconceivable in other more densely-populated nations.*

106-107 *The whole nation is proud of its beauty queens and two Miss Worlds were born in Iceland.*

Young adults, the future of the nation

108-109 *The birth-rate is quite high in Iceland and infant mortality is the lowest in the world. The adults treat children almost as equals and, on the whole, they are not at all spoilt; they are the object of the love and attention of the entire community. Young Icelanders are resolute and extremely independent from a young age, partly because everyone is very attentive to their safety. Publications intended for tourists, for instance, usually contain*

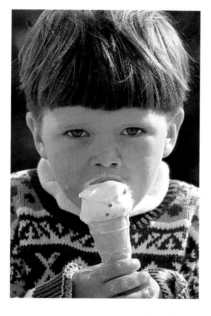

a warning that goes more or less like this: "Icelandic children spend a great deal of time playing in the open air: if you are driving you must expect to encounter children playing anywhere and at any time". The last specification is explained by the fact that the night in summer is non-existent and so even at late hours groups of children can be seen enjoying the warm air and a few precious rays of sun. On the whole, Icelandic society is very informal and egalitarian: practically everyone loves children and will do their best to welcome them into society as best they can, whether brought up in a normal family or living with just one parent. It is no surprise therefore that "unmarried mothers" or "unmarried fathers" are not at all stigmatised - after all the children are the future and the wealth of the country.

Active, proud and dynamic

110 top and 110-111 A typical trait of the Icelandic character is activity, intended in the most energetic sense. Participation in cultural and social events - including the annual "Herring festival" seen here in full swing - is very high even though Icelanders have less spare time than the inhabitants of many other nations. This country has the longest work hours in Europe, necessary to obtain all the material benefits that have become so greatly desired by modern society.

110 centre left The Viking origins of the Icelandic people are commemorated by a group of actors in the port of Hafnarfjördur, near Reykjavík.

110 centre right This girl proudly wears the national costume; in Iceland there is still a strong bond between past and present.

110 bottom The most important celebrations for the National festival on 17th June are held in Reykjavik with parades, street concerts, dancing and public performances. Popular participation is practically total and very enthusiastic.

112-113 Icelanders live in towns that have maintained a human dimension (the picture shows Akureyri) and the children still have room to play.

Sheep, a controversial wealth

114 top   *Poor soil and low temperatures have made stockbreeding, especially that of horses and sheep, more important than agriculture.*
The meadows and pastures that cover 22 per cent of the national territory feed large numbers of animals and a tenth of the population is involved in sheep-rearing or in the textile industries that process wool.

114 bottom   *The children that live in the farms scattered along the coasts are accustomed to bleating sheep. The Icelandic farmers have always been dedicated mostly to sheep-farming because this land was traditionally used only to cultivate potatoes, cabbages or carrots. Only in recent years have they used the hot springs and constructed greenhouses in which to grow fruit and vegetables.*

114-115 *At the end of the summer the sheep are gathered in large circular pens such as that seen here at Midfjördur and returned to their legitimate owners on the basis of an identification sign that each animal has on its ear. Although Icelandic society is becoming rapidly more urbanised and the country lives mainly off fishing, its approximately 800,000 sheep are a considerable wealth. On the other hand, because left free to graze everywhere, they represent a serious obstacle to the development of flora and make vast reforestation work very difficult. Iceland has not always been so barren; trees were felled in large numbers by the Vikings who needed wood to construct houses and boats.*

115 right *The wool produced is one of the softest in the world, with far longer fibres than other types and very waterproof: in fact Icelandic sweaters are quite famous. Typical ones have traditional geometric designs and are made with wool that is not coloured artificially, thus conserving the natural hues of the fleece.*

Fish and more fish

116 top and bottom left *There is something unreal about this fishing boat photographed in the port of Búdir, transported on a trolley and surrounded by a mass of brightly-coloured buoys. The Icelandic economy still gravitates greatly around fishing and related industries; only in the last few decades has there been a considerable boost to diversified industrial activities and the exportation of products such as wool, leather, diatomite and materials for building.*

116 right *The Icelandic winner of the Nobel Prize for Literature, Halldór Laxness one day spoke words that made history: "For Iceland, life is dried cod". This is still very true even though in place of the dried cod today there is fresh or frozen fish. Nonetheless it is still quite common on the island to see the racks used to hang out the cod to dry; not even the heads are wasted: they are exported to some African countries.*

117 *One activity still at the experimental stage but which has produced encouraging results is the sea farming of salmon. The picture shows an expert at work near Höfn and is a reminder that Iceland is a country where male and female equality is no dream, but has deep roots.*

118-119 *The arrival of freshly-caught fish in the port of Höfn is a sight that is repeated every day and means prosperity for the whole community. Fishing absorbs only 12 per cent of the work force in Iceland but produces 75 per cent of the national product. This country boasts an avant-garde fishing fleet but has, in recent years, had to face worrying reductions in the cod and herring shoals, adopting protection measures that have not failed to stir controversy.*

120-121 *Pure, crystal-clear water, practically free from pollution, has always made Iceland a paradise for angling enthusiasts. In the rivers and lakes of Iceland - this is the Veidivötn - fishermen catch huge trout and some of the most prized salmon in the world.*

Sports for all tastes

122 *Clean air and spectacular scenery make Iceland the ideal place for open-air sports, mountaineering included. Although the island's mountains are not that high, the latitude makes everything more difficult - here the glaciers start at sea level!*

122 centre *As in all north European countries, ice hockey is particularly popular and the national team have a highly respectable record for such a small population. Icelanders are particularly good at sports in which strength and resistance count most, which is only natural because their race is perhaps the biggest in the world. The average male height is 5 feet 8 inches and the weight exceeds the European standard by about 9 pounds.*

122 bottom *Considering all its players are amateurs, the national football team has earned itself a good international reputation. Not every day does a dentist take up his position in goal or a postman play centre forward.*

122-123 *One sport that has become increasingly popular in recent years is rafting, the exciting descent of watercourses in dinghies; when practised in rivers with particularly strong currents and numerous rapids this is extremely testing, even for the most skilled.*

124 *For Icelanders, swimming is more than a sport, it is a national aptitude, a vital activity both for health and for personal safety and an obligatory subject in the school curriculum. This attitude is quite understandable in a society that, until very recently, was profoundly bound to life on the sea; moreover, the frequent presence of warm thermal springs (seen here at Laufafell) makes contact with the water decidedly pleasant.*

125 top *Canoes are an original and fascinating way to see Iceland, whether along the coasts of the fjords or on inland rivers. The unique routes and the majestic scenery transform even a short trip into an unforgettable experience, on the condition that caution is taken and safety equipment used at all times. Although splendid Nature in Iceland does not permit carelessness, it demands admiration and respect.*

125 bottom *The most attractive feature of the numerous Icelandic swimming pools is hot water all year round supplied by geothermal springs at a temperature between 61 F and 146 F. For this reason the fact that nearly all swimming pools are in the open air is no deterrent to the locals - though it is for most tourists - not even in the middle of winter; indeed for many the main attraction of a dive lies in the contrast between warm water and freezing cold air.*

In Iceland even horses are special

126 top left *Icelandic horses, thickset and sturdy, descend directly from those imported to the island by the Viking settlers in the 10th century. The island's geographic isolation has protected them from crossbreeding and now there are approximately 65,000, half of which live partially wild. Strong, affectionate and obstinate, the Icelandic horse was for centuries vitally important in a country that until the 19th century almost totally lacked roads.*

126 top right *Riding is the best-loved sport of the Icelandic people and they devote themselves to it from infancy; all over the island there are dozens of clubs and the whole summer sees competitions, fairs and shows. The Icelandic breed is protected by severe regulations and it is forbidden to import any other horse for fear of introducing illnesses to which the local animals are not immune.*

126 bottom *This is by no means a rare sight even today in Iceland: horses continue to perform numerous tasks in the rural areas.*

126-127 *The love of the Icelandic people for riding and open-air adventure knows no bounds. Numerous farms offer horse treks and these can last from an hour to ten days.*

128 *Flaming-red walls, flowers in full view, windows framed with delicate, hand-embroidered curtains; anyone who has just once enjoyed traditional Icelandic hospitality knows that sooner or later he must return to the island of the icy face and fiery heart.*